Hip Hop

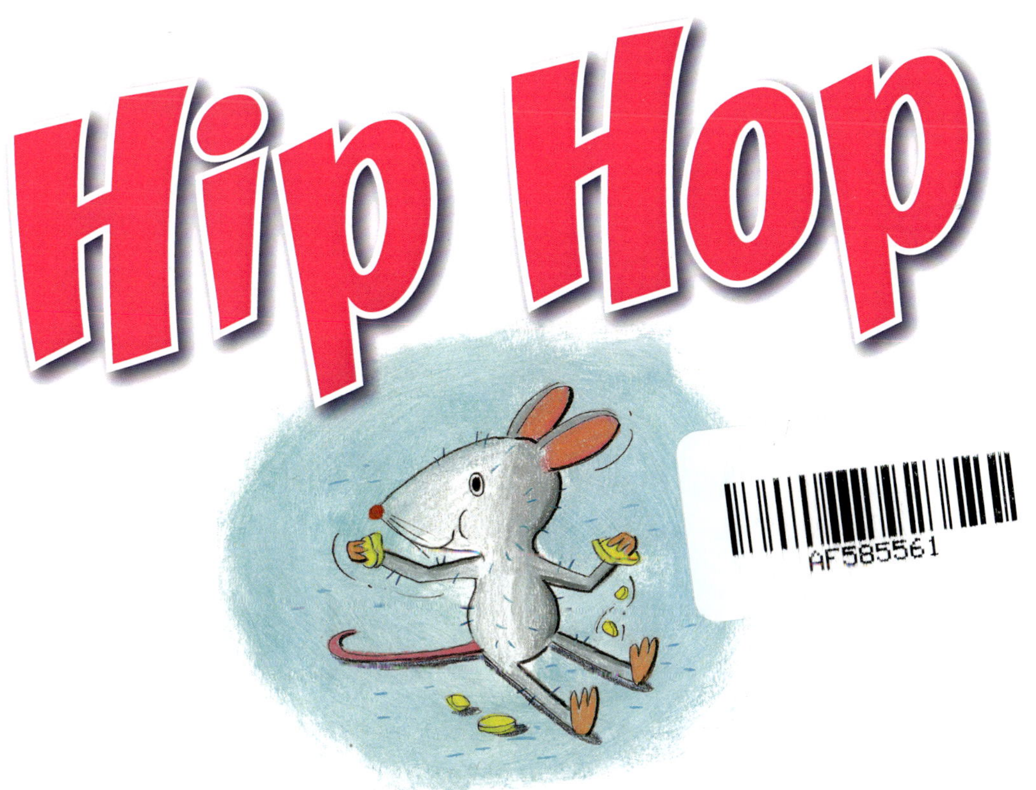

Jane Langford

Illustrated by Christina Bretschneider

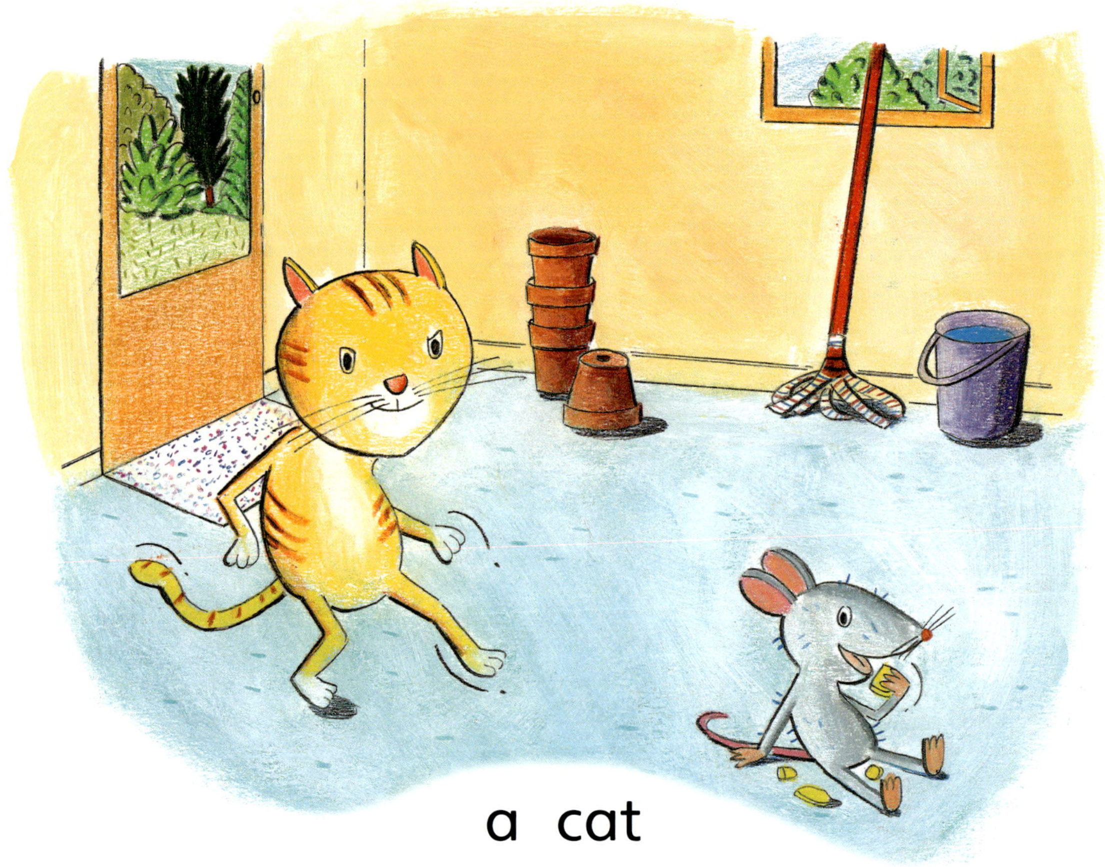

a cat

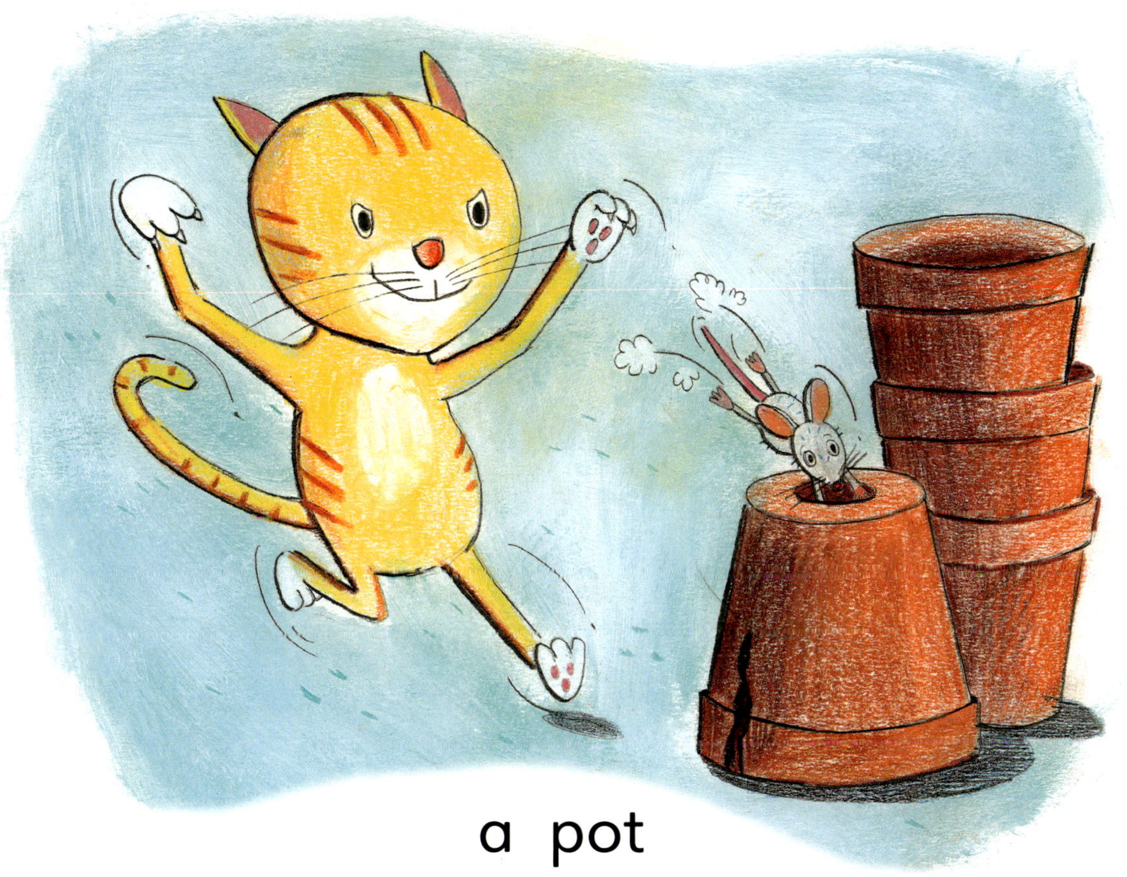

a pot

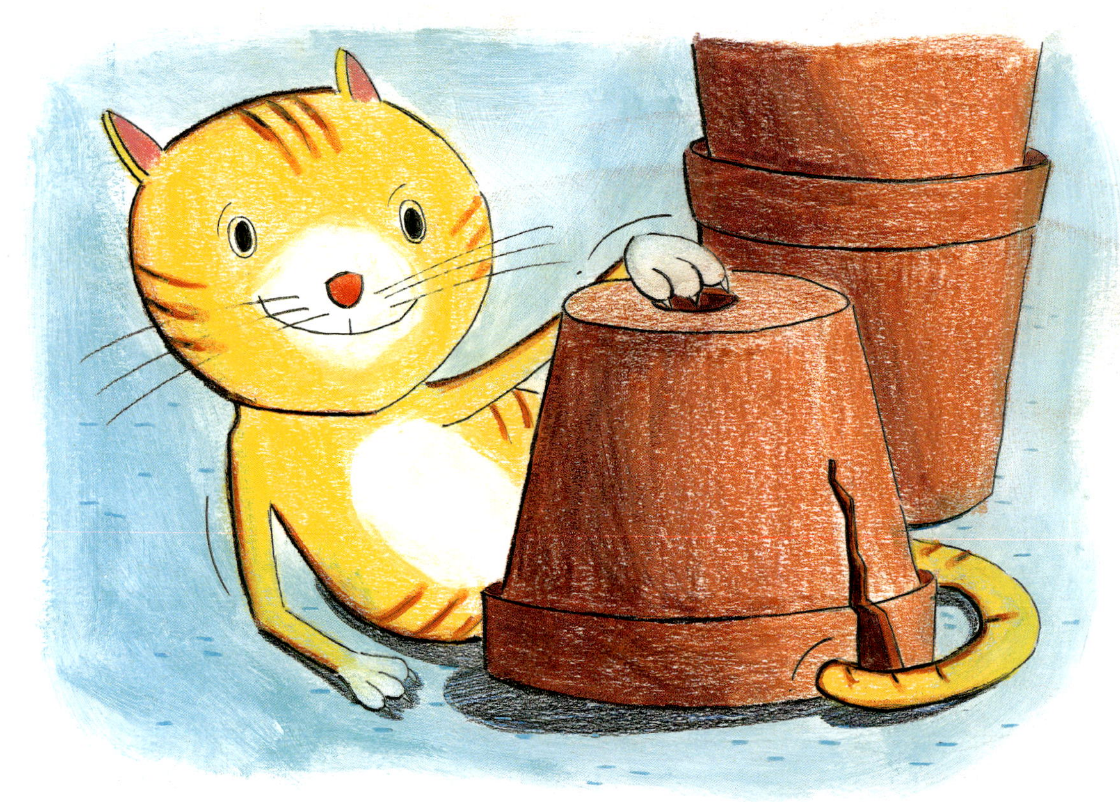

a pat and a tap

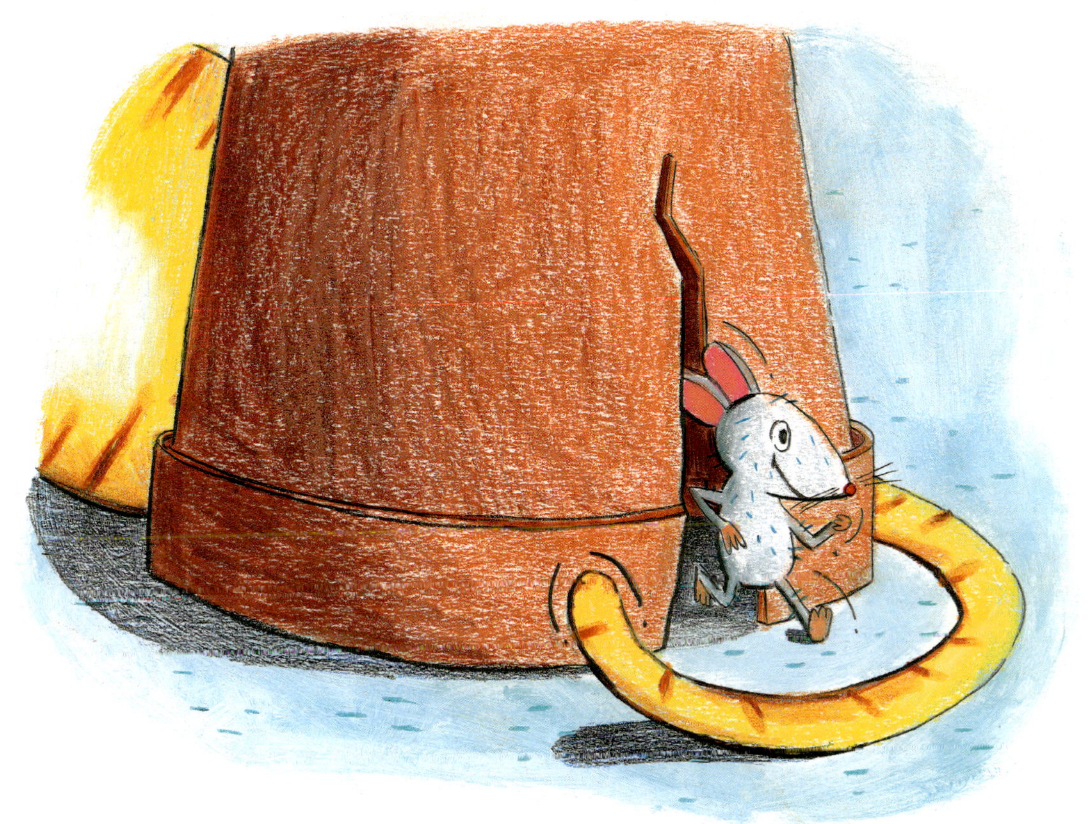

a gap

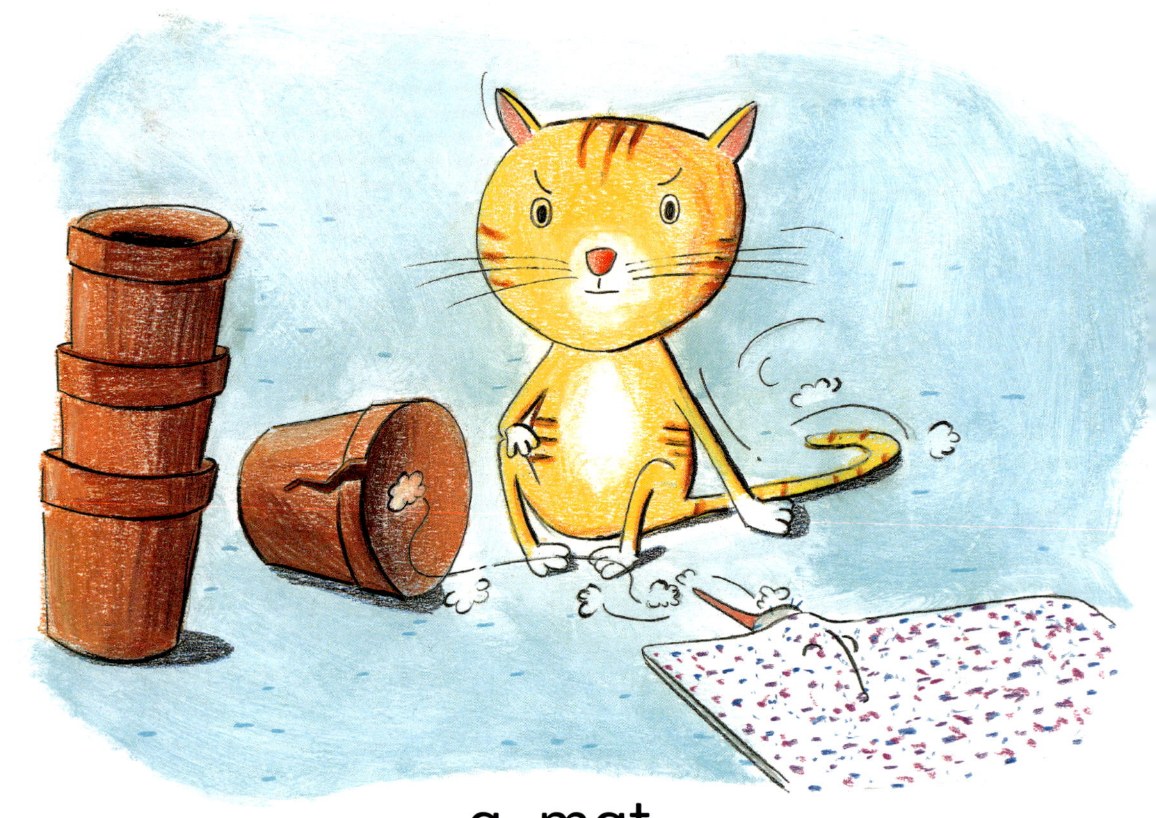

a mat

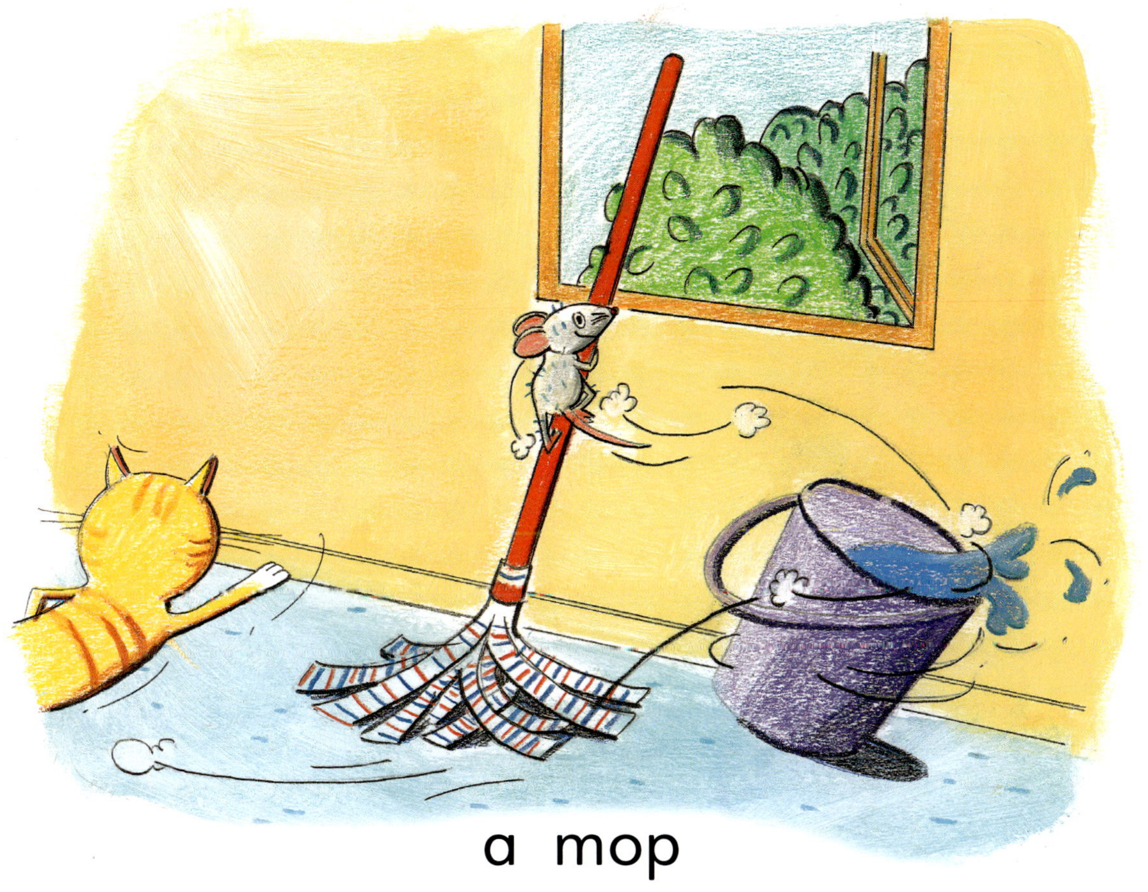

a mop

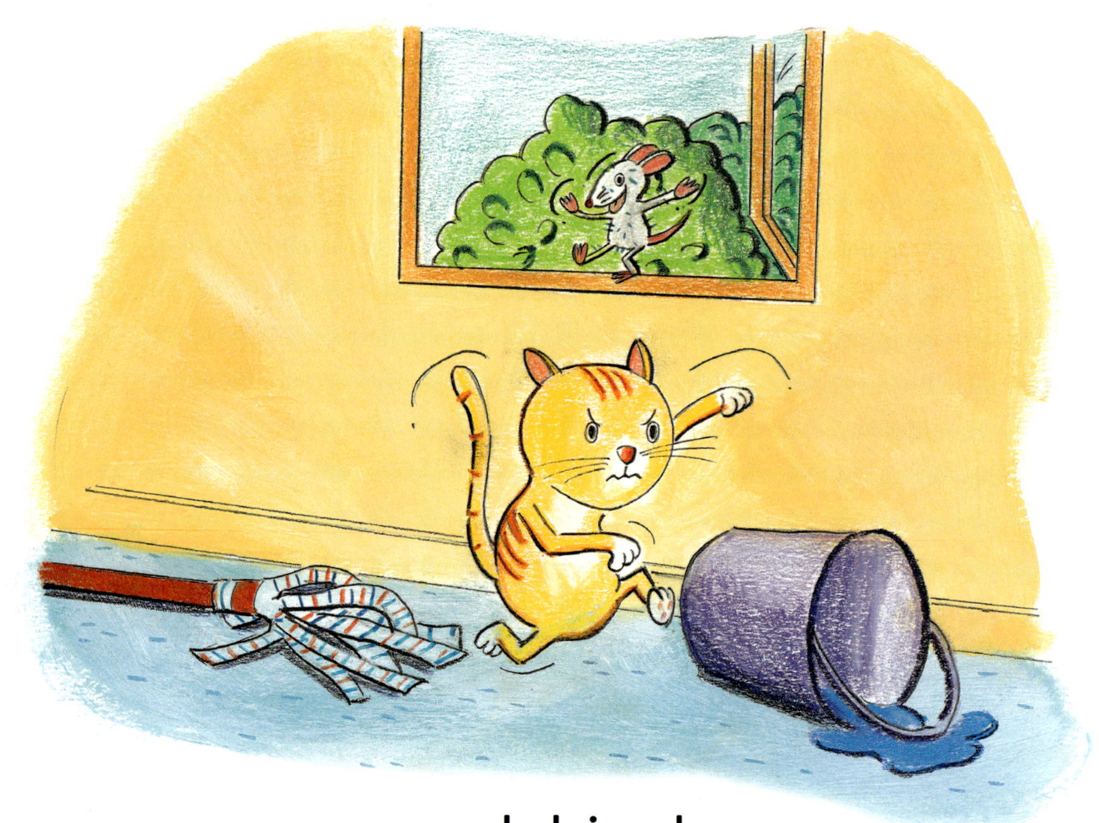

a mad hip hop